KEEP THE FLAG FLYING

KEEP THE FLAG FLYING
KEEP THE FLAG FLYING
KEEP THE FLAG FLYING
KEEP THE FLAG FLYING
KEEP THE FLAG FLYING
KEEP THE FLAG FLYING
KEEP THE FLAG FLYING
KEEP THE FLAG FLYING

KEEP
THE
FLAG
FLYING

KEEP
THE
FLAG
FLYING

KEEP
THE
FLAG
FLYING

KEEP
THE
FLAG
FLYING

KEEP
THE
FLAG
FLYING

KEEP
THE
FLAG
FLYING

KEEP
THE
FLAG
FLYING

KEEP
THE
FLAG
FLYING

KEEP
THE
FLAG
FLYING

KEEP THE FLAG FLYING

Copyright © Summersdale Publishers Ltd, 2012

All rights reserved.

Summersdale Publishers Ltd
46 West Street
Chichester
West Sussex
PO19 1RP
UK

www.summersdale.com

Printed and bound in the Czech Republic

ISBN: 978-1-84953-268-6

Substantial discounts on bulk quantities of Summersdale books are available to corporations, professional associations and other organisations. For details telephone Summersdale Publishers on (+44-1243-771107), fax (+44-1243-786300) or email (nicky@summersdale.com).

KEEP
THE
FLAG
FLYING

However British you
may be, I am more
British still.

Henry James

The British have a
remarkable talent for
keeping calm, even when
there is no crisis.

Franklin P. Jones

The gentleness of the English civilisation is perhaps its most marked characteristic. You notice it the moment you set foot on English soil.

George Orwell

The British nation is unique… They are the only people who like to be told how bad things are, who like to be told the worst.

Winston Churchill

I had the patriotic conviction that... there was almost nothing that the British people could not do.

Margaret Thatcher

The British electors
will not vote for a man
who doesn't wear
a hat.

Lord Beaverbrook

Be Like Dad:
Keep Mum!

World War Two slogan

Thank God for tea! What
would the world do without
tea? How did it exist? I am
glad I was not born
before tea.

Reverend Sydney Smith

... tea is one of the
main stays of civilization
in this country.

**George Orwell,
'A Nice Cup of Tea'**

Heaven take my soul,
and England keep
my bones!

William Shakespeare, *King John*

We English are good at
forgiving our enemies;
it releases us from the
obligation of liking
our friends.

P. D. James

The noblest
prospect which a
Scotchman ever sees
is the high-road that
leads him to England.

Samuel Johnson

But it is my happiness
to be half Welsh, and
that the better half.

Richard Cobden

No one can be as
calculatedly rude as the
British, which amazes
Americans, who do not
understand studied insult
and can only offer abuse
as a substitute.

Paul Gallico

I hope for nothing in this world so ardently as once again to see that paradise called England.

Cosimo III,
Grand Duke of Tuscany

Back up the Fighting Forces

World War Two slogan

The English Winter –
ending in July,
To recommence
in August.

Lord Byron

It is commonly observed, that when two Englishmen meet, their first talk is of the weather; they are in haste to tell each other, what each must already know, that it is hot or cold, bright or cloudy, windy or calm.

Samuel Johnson

Summer afternoon –
summer afternoon; to me
those have always been the
most beautiful words in the
English language.

Henry James

You often hear that the English climate has had a profound effect upon the English temperament. I don't believe it. I believe they were always like that.

Will Cuppy

'You might, from your appearance, be the wife of Lucifer,' said Miss Pross, in her breathing. 'Nevertheless, you shall not get the better of me. I am an Englishwoman.'

Charles Dickens, *A Tale of Two Cities*

The English have an
extraordinary ability
for flying into a
great calm.

Alexander Woollcott

Well, I'm having a good time. Which makes me feel guilty too. How very English.

David Attenborough

The English never
draw a line without
blurring it.

Winston Churchill

Careless Talk
Costs Lives!

World War Two slogan

The roots and herbes
beaten and put into new Ale
or Beer, and daily drank,
cleareth, strengtheneth and
quickeneth the sight of
the eyes…

Nicholas Culpeper,
The English Physician

In my opinion, most of the great men of the past were only there for the beer.

A. J. P. Taylor

What two ideas are
more inseparable than
Beer and Britannia?

Reverend Sydney Smith

In the fell clutch of circumstance
I have not winced nor cried aloud.
Under the bludgeonings of chance
My head is bloody, but unbowed.

**William Ernest Henley,
from 'Invictus'**

The English
instinctively admire
any man who has no
talent, and is modest
about it.

James Agate

Dig For Victory

World War Two slogan

It is equality of monotony which makes the strength of the British Isles.

Eleanor Roosevelt

My theory is that all of Scottish cuisine is based on a dare.

Mike Myers

The Welsh are so damn
Welsh that it looks
like affectation.

Alexander Raleigh

I like the English.
They have the
most rigid code of
immorality in
the world.

Malcolm Bradbury

The English are not very
spiritual people, so they
invented cricket to give them
some idea of eternity.

George Bernard Shaw

What a pity it is
that we have no
amusements in
England but vice
and religion!

Reverend Sydney Smith

If you can fill the
unforgiving minute
With sixty seconds' worth
of distance run,
Yours is the Earth and
everything that's in it,
And – which is more – you'll
be a Man, my son!

Rudyard Kipling, from 'If –'

Death seems to provide the
minds of the Anglo-Saxon
race with a greater fund of
amusement than any other
single subject.

Dorothy L. Sayers

Freedom Is
In Peril:
Defend It with
All Your Might

World War Two slogan

We know no spectacle so
ridiculous as the British
public in one of its periodical
fits of morality.

Thomas B. Macaulay

If I am pushed I will
push back, that is the
way I am. I am
very British.

Damon Hill

Fortunately in England, at any rate, education produces no effect whatsoever. If it did, it would prove a serious danger to the upper classes, and probably lead to acts of violence in Grosvenor Square.

Oscar Wilde,
The Importance of Being Earnest

The English have all the material requisites for the revolution. What they lack is the spirit of generalisation and revolutionary ardour.

Karl Marx

The Irish and British,
they love satire, it's
a large part of
the culture.

Ben Nicholson

I got into my bones the
essential structure of the
ordinary British sentence –
which is a noble thing.

Winston Churchill

King Louis Philippe once
said to me that he attributed
the great success of the
British nation in political life
to their talking politics
after dinner.

Benjamin Disraeli

Together For Victory

World War Two slogan

We don't take ourselves as seriously as some other countries do.

Joan Collins

Foreigners may pretend
otherwise, but if English
is spoken loudly enough,
anyone can understand it,
the British included.

P. J. O'Rourke

… life is unliveable to
them unless they have
tea and puddings.

George Orwell on the English

Under certain circumstances
there are few hours in
life more agreeable than
the hour dedicated to
the ceremony known as
afternoon tea.

Henry James, *The Portrait of a Lady*

Theirs not to make reply,
Theirs not to reason why,
Theirs but to do and die.
Into the valley of Death
Rode the six hundred.

**Alfred, Lord Tennyson, from
'The Charge of the Light Brigade'**

Now order the ranks, and
fling wide the banners, for
our souls are God's and our
bodies the king's, and our
swords for Saint George
and for England!

Sir Arthur Conan Doyle,
The White Company

Continental people
have sex-lives;
the English have
hot-water bottles.

George Mikes

I am not an Englishman,
I was never an Englishman,
and I don't ever want to be
one. I am a Scotsman!
I was a Scotsman and I will
always be one.

Sean Connery

To be born in Wales…
with music in your blood
and with poetry in your soul,
is a privilege indeed.

Brian Harris

Lend a Hand
on the Land

World War Two slogan

Let us therefore brace ourselves to our duty, and so bear ourselves that if the British Empire and its Commonwealth last for a thousand years, men will still say, 'This was their finest hour.'

Winston Churchill

The English may
not always be the
best writers in the
world, but they are
incomparably the best
dull writers.

Raymond Chandler

The English never smash in a face. They merely refrain from asking it to dinner.

Margaret Halsey

Only England could have
produced him, and he
always said that the country
was going to the dogs. His
principles were out of date,
but there was a good deal to
be said for his prejudices.

**Oscar Wilde describing Lord
Fermor in *The Picture of Dorian Gray***

The English are
predisposed to pride,
the French to vanity.

Jean-Jacques Rousseau

It only takes a room of
Americans for the English
and Australians to realise
how much we have
in common.

Stephen Fry

Tea's proper use is to
amuse the idle, and relax
the studious, and dilute
the full meals of those who
cannot use exercise, and
will not use abstinence.

Samuel Johnson

Tea to the English is
really a picnic indoors.

Alice Walker

Our trouble is that we drink too much tea.

J. B. Priestley

A hardened and shameless
tea-drinker... who with tea
amused the evening, with
tea solaced the midnight,
and with tea welcomed
the morning.

Samuel Johnson describing himself

On the Continent
people have good food; in
England people have good
table manners.

George Mikes

Your Britain:
Fight for it Now!

World War Two slogan

I see the damage done
by enemy attacks; but I
also see… the spirit of an
unconquerable people.

Winston Churchill

This England never
did, nor never shall,
Lie at the proud foot
of a conqueror.

William Shakespeare, *King John*

Whatever there is in
the English character of
persistence, obstinacy,
patience, industry, sobriety,
love of freedom, we are
accustomed to attribute to
our Anglo-Saxon descent.

Walter Besant, *The History of London*

The proper means of
increasing the love
we bear our native
country is to reside
some time in a
foreign one.

William Shenstone

The whole strength of
England lies in the fact that
the enormous majority of the
English people are snobs.

George Bernard Shaw

The Irish gave the bagpipes to the Scots as a joke, but the Scots haven't seen the joke yet.

Oliver Herford

Each section of the British Isles has its own way of laughing, except Wales, which doesn't.

Stephen Leacock

I see you stand like greyhounds in the slips,
Straining upon the start. The game's afoot:
Follow your spirit; and upon this charge
Cry 'God for Harry, England and Saint George!'

William Shakespeare, *Henry V*

By the by, if the English race
had done nothing else, yet if
they left the world the notion
of a gentleman, they would
have done a great service
to mankind.

Gerard Manley Hopkins

Everything depends on whether we have for opponents those French tricksters or those daring rascals, the English. I prefer the English.

**Manfred von Richthofen
(The Red Baron)**

<u>Your</u> Courage
<u>Your</u> Cheerfulness
<u>Your</u> Resolution
Will Bring Us Victory

World War Two slogan

The difference between
the vanity of a Frenchman
and an Englishman seems
to be this: The one thinks
everything right that is
French, the other thinks
everything wrong that is
not English.

William Hazlitt

To Americans, English
manners are far more
frightening than none at all.

Randall Jarrell

'Sybil has an English heart, and that's not easily broken.'

Benjamin Disraeli, *Sybil*

... be England what she will,
With all her faults, she is my
country still.

**Charles Churchill, from
'The Farewell'**

I know I have the body of
a weak and feeble woman,
but I have the heart and
stomach of a king, and of a
king of England, too.

Elizabeth I

There is a forgotten, nay
almost forbidden word,
which means more to me
than any other. That word
is England.

Winston Churchill

The Englishman has
all the qualities of
a poker except its
occasional warmth.

Daniel O'Connell

England is unrivalled
for two things – sport
and politics.

Benjamin Disraeli

By this sacredness of individuals, the English have in seven hundred years evolved the principles of freedom.

Ralph Waldo Emerson

Tittle Tattle
Lost the Battle

World War Two slogan

I think the British have the distinction above all other nations of being able to put new wine into old bottles without bursting them.

Clement Attlee

We'll drink off the liquor
while we can stand,
And hey for the honour of
old England!

From 'Harvest-Home Song',
an old English ballad

No soldier can fight
unless he is properly
fed on beef and beer.

**John Churchill,
First Duke of Marlborough**

They are like their own beer;
froth on top, dregs at bottom,
the middle excellent.

Voltaire on the British

This blessed plot,
this earth, this realm,
this England.

William Shakespeare, *Richard II*

If I should die, think only
this of me:
That there's some corner
of a foreign field
That is forever England.

Rupert Brooke, from 'The Soldier'

An Englishman, even
if he is alone, forms
an orderly queue
of one.

George Mikes

In truth, no men on earth
can cheer like Englishmen,
who do so rally one
another's blood and spirit
when they cheer in earnest,
that the stir is like the rush
of their whole history…

Charles Dickens, *Little Dorrit*

Go Through Your Wardrobe – Make-do and Mend

World War Two slogan

The basis of English
morality is Insight.
With insight you may
go far and do great
things: but you must
walk by faith.

George Unwin

Ask any man what
nationality he would prefer
to be, and ninety-nine out of
a hundred will tell you that
they would prefer to
be Englishmen.

Cecil Rhodes

A young Scotsman of your
ability let loose upon the
world with £300, what
could he not do? It's
almost appalling to think of;
especially if he went among
the English.

J. M. Barrie,
What Every Woman Knows

The Welsh are all
actors. It's only the
bad ones who become
professional.

Richard Burton

Never ask a man if he's from Yorkshire. If he is, he'll already have told you. If he isn't, why embarrass him?

Roy Hattersley

Would I were in an
alehouse in London!
I would give
all my fame for a pot
of ale and safety.

William Shakespeare, *Henry V*

Good ale, the true and proper drink of Englishmen. He is not deserving of the name of Englishman who speaketh against ale, that is good ale.

George Borrow, *Lavengro*

Waste the Food
and
Help the Hun

World War Two slogan

… a polite public will no more bear to read an authentic description of vice than a truly refined English or American female will permit the word breeches to be pronounced in her chaste hearing.

W. M. Thackeray, *Vanity Fair*

England expects
every man will do
his duty.

Admiral Horatio Nelson

There is nothing about
which I am more anxious
than my country, and for its
sake I am willing to die ten
deaths, if that be possible.

Elizabeth I

In England every man ought to own a garden. It's meant to be that way, you feel it immediately.

Henry Miller

I shall not cease from
mental fight,
Nor shall my sword sleep in
my hand,
Till we have built Jerusalem
In England's green and
pleasant land.

William Blake, from 'Jerusalem'

The national sport of
England is obstacle-racing.
People fill their rooms with
useless and cumbersome
furniture, and spend the rest
of their lives in trying
to dodge it.

Herbert Beerbohm Tree

The land of embarrassment and breakfast.

Julian Barnes on Britain

We must be free or die,
who speak the tongue
That Shakespeare spoke:
the faith and morals hold
Which Milton held.

**William Wordsworth, from 'We
Must Be Free or Die'**

Holding the Line!

World War Two slogan

In peacetime the British may have many faults; but so far an inferiority complex has not been one of them.

Lord Gladwyn

And though hard be
the task, 'Keep a stiff
upper lip.'

Phoebe Cary

The English
countryside is the
most staggeringly
beautiful place.

Guy Ritchie

When it's three o'clock
in New York, it's still
1938 in London.

Bette Midler

How amazing that the language of a few thousand savages living on a fog-encrusted island in the North Sea should become the language of the world.

Norman St John-Stevas

But, after all, what would the English be without their sweet unreasonableness?

John Galsworthy

There is nothing so bad or
so good that you will not
find Englishmen doing it;
but you will never find an
Englishman in the wrong.
He does everything
on principle.

George Bernard Shaw,
The Man of Destiny

I don't like England very much, but the English *do* seem rather lovable people. They have such a lot of gentleness.

D. H. Lawrence

I fall in love with
Britain every day, with
bridges, buses,
blue skies…

Pete Doherty

Thou Saint George shalt
called bee,
Saint George of mery
England, the signe
of victoree.

Edmund Spenser, from
'The Faerie Queen'

Coughs and Sneezes
Spread Diseases

World War Two slogan

The best thing I know
between France and
England is the sea.

Douglas Jerrold

There are still parts of Wales
where the only concession
to gaiety is a striped shroud.

Gwyn Thomas

An Englishman is a man
who lives on an island in the
North Sea governed
by Scotsmen.

Philip Guedalla

It profits a man
nothing to give his
soul for the whole
world… but for Wales!

Robert Bolt

But we are the people of England; and we have not spoken yet.
Smile at us, pay us, pass us. But do not quite forget.

G. K. Chesterton, from
'The Secret People'

If an Englishman gets
run down by a truck,
he apologizes to
the truck.

Jackie Mason

I feel in regard to this aged England… that she sees a little better on a cloudy day and that, in storm of battle and calamity, she has a secret vigour and a pulse like a cannon.

Ralph Waldo Emerson

We beat 'em before –
We will beat 'em again

World War Two slogan

Ever the faith endures,
England, my England.

W. E. Henley

Other nations use force –
we Britons alone use Might.

Evelyn Waugh

A Nation not slow and dull,
but of quick, ingenious,
and piercing spirit, acute to
invent, suttle and sinewy
to discours, not beneath
the reach of any point
the highest that humane
capacity can soar to.

**John Milton describing England
in *Areopagitica***

An Englishman, being
flattered, is a lamb;
threatened, a lion.

George Chapman

The place was so
British I wouldn't be
surprised if the mice
wore monocles.

Bob Hope

Our true Patron Saint is
not St George but Sir John
Falstaff... we are the most
civilised people in the world,
the reason being that we are
the most humorous people
in the world.

Hesketh Pearson, *The English Genius*

If you want to eat well
in England, eat three
breakfasts.

W. Somerset Maugham

Freedom Will Prevail

World War Two slogan

I'm very proud to be British, and my brand is British.

Victoria Beckham

The English may not like
music – but they absolutely
love the noise it makes.

Sir Thomas Beecham

To be an Englishman
is to belong to the
most exclusive club
there is.

Ogden Nash

England has saved herself
by her exertions, and will, as
I trust, save Europe by
her example.

William Pitt

Always remember that you are an Englishman and therefore have drawn the first prize in the lottery of life.

Cecil Rhodes

What is our task?
To make Britain a fit
country for heroes
to live in.

David Lloyd George

England! my country,
great and free!
Heart of the world,
I leap to thee!

Philip James Bailey

Let Us Go
Forward Together

World War Two slogan

BAKE FOR BRITAIN

£4.99

ISBN: 978 1 84953 267 9

*'The most sincere love of all
is the love of food.'*

George Bernard Shaw

TASTY ADVICE FOR BRITISH BAKERS

Sumptuous scones with jam and clotted cream, lemon drizzle cake, Victoria sponge and brandy snaps – just a few of the sweet treats that get British taste buds tingling. So put on your apron, dig out the mixing bowl and start the oven because it's time to go baking mad.

Here's a book packed with recipes and quotations to help you bake your country proud.

NOW
PANIC
AND
FREAK
OUT

NOW PANIC AND FREAK OUT

£4.99

ISBN: 978 1 84953 103 0

'*We experience moments absolutely free from worry. These brief respites are called panic.*'

Cullen Hightower

BAD ADVICE FOR GOOD PEOPLE

Keep Calm and Carry On is all very well, but life just isn't that simple. Let's own up and face facts: we're getting older, the politicians are not getting any wiser, and the world's going to hell in a handbasket.

It's time to panic.

Here's a book packed with quotations proving that keeping calm is simply not an option.

www.summersdale.com